12 Steps To Greatness

Keys to Unlocking Your Potential For A Life Of Fulfillment And Success

Victoria Simeon

TABLE OF CONTENTS

INTRODUCTION

The future is bright with possibilities, but if we don't take advantage of them now they will pass us by without us even noticing them at all.

It's our job as individuals to find ways to turn those possibilities into realities through hard work and determination! Instead of focusing on what is wrong, We should focus on finding answers for how things can be improved or changed.

There was a young lady named Naomi. She was a hardworking and ambitious woman who had big dreams of becoming great in life.

Naomi had a plan to achieve her goals. She was determined to make something of herself, so she began setting small goals for herself each day.

She would wake up early in the morning to get a head start on her day and took classes to improve her skills and knowledge.

Naomi also took steps to improve her communication and leadership skills. She joined a number of clubs and societies where she could practice her public speaking and leadership skills. She also took part in many volunteer activities to help her network and build relationships with people who could help her reach her goals.

She also started networking with other successful people in her field, attending conferences and seminars to broaden her perspectives. Naomi also read lots of books and took notes to stay up-to-date with the latest trends.

In addition, Naomi kept a daily journal to document her progress and set new goals for herself. She also made sure to take care of her mental and physical health by exercising, getting enough sleep, and eating healthy.

Finally, Naomi never gave up. She kept pushing herself to be the best she could be, no matter what happened. She was often told that her dreams were impossible, but she didn't let that stop her.

Years passed and soon enough, Naomi had achieved her goals and was now a successful businesswoman. She had earned respect and admiration from those around her and was living her best life.

Greatness is the quality of being distinguished or exceptional in some way. It is a broad term that can be applied to many different aspects of life, from moral or physical courage to leadership, creativity, or intellectual achievement.

Greatness is a feeling that is hard to define and measure. It is something that is often sought after but rarely achieved. It is a feeling of accomplishment and pride.
 It is a sense of being the best at something, or of having achieved something that is difficult or remarkable.

Greatness can be seen in people who have made an impact on the world, such as Nelson Mandela, Mark Zuckerberg, Martin Luther King, Jr., Mother Teresa, Kamala Harris, Rosa Parks and Maya Angelou.
It can also be seen in people who have achieved great success in their chosen field, such as Steve Jobs and Bill Gates.

Greatness can also be seen in everyday people who go beyond what is expected of them. People who take the time to help those in need, or to volunteer in their community. People who put in the hard work and dedication to achieve something that is difficult and rewarding. People who strive for excellence in their chosen profession.

Greatness is not something that can be quantified or measured. It is a feeling that comes from within and is unique to each individual. It is something that can be admired and respected, but never truly achieved. It is a feeling that can inspire others to do great things and be the best that they can be.

Have you ever felt like you wanted to make a change in your life or reach a certain goal, but you weren't sure how to get there? If so, you're not alone.

Many of us struggle to know where to start when we want to make a change or achieve something great. The good news is that there is a path to greatness, and you can find it here. These steps will provide you with the direction and motivation you need to make the changes you desire and achieve the success you've been dreaming of.

This is a path to discovering the greatness within you and releasing it out into the world. This program will provide you with the tools to help you grow and develop into a more successful and well-rounded individual.

Through this program, you will be able to identify your strengths and weaknesses, and use them to your advantage. You will also learn how to set attainable goals and create a plan to reach them.

With some practical examples, you will learn how to unlock your greatness and transform your life. You will be empowered to reach your potential and become the very best version of yourself.

So, if you are ready to embark on this journey, let's get started on the path to unlocking greatness.

YOU ARE CAPABLE
OF GREATNESS

1.

BECOME ANGRY

Your future is shaped by your present-day intolerance. The first step to greatness is to become upset with your current circumstances. Until you become irritated, nothing happens! It won't change if you can live with it.

Intolerance of your current circumstance may spur you to make adjustments that result in a better future. You can channel this energy to find solutions and implement changes that will pave the way for a better future if you are frustrated and unsatisfied with the way things are right now.

You can adopt new ways of thinking or engage in various behaviors to help you build the future you want.

According to the proverb, "what you focus on grows."
Lack of desire and a significant deal of dissatisfaction can result from intolerance of your current circumstance. Focusing on the negative aspects of your current circumstance might cause dissatisfaction and a sense of helplessness.

On the other hand, you may improve your future for yourself if you concentrate on what you can do to make your present position better. This could entail devising a strategy to achieve your objectives, acting, or adopting an optimistic outlook. By taking charge of your current position, you may shape a better future with persistent effort and determination.

Get Angry and say to yourself

I'm sick of feeling helpless. I've been trying very hard to advance in life, yet all I seem to be doing is standing still.

I'm irritated and angry with how things are right now, but I won't let that anger win; instead, I'll use it as fuel to achieve greatness.

I'm tired of having the feeling that I'm not achieving my full potential. It's time for a change because I'm sick of using all the justifications to avoid acting.

I'll concentrate on identifying solutions for how things might be modified or improved. I will take action every single day, no matter how tiny a step it may be, to build a brighter future for myself.

I won't settle for anything less than what I know I'm capable of. No more settling for mediocrity or playing small; stop letting doubt or fear prevent me from achieving my goals. It's time for me to act and take charge of my life so that I may do more! Instead of yelling at other people, I want to use my rage to do action that will lead to greatness.

Now, instead of being an anchor holding you down, your negative emotions are being channeled into motivation.

Realizing that your current situation is keeping you from realizing your dreams frustrates you, but it also makes you stronger and wiser. Now is the time to act; this is the time when everything will change!

The possibilities in the future are great, but if we don't seize them now, they will pass us by without us even realizing them. It is up to each of us to use our own creativity to find methods to make those opportunities a reality.

The task at hand is difficult, but it's essential if you want to realize your full potential and work toward success in your personal and professional endeavors. Whatever difficulties you may face in the future will seem small in comparison to your inner strength, which is ready to overcome any challenges that may arise. Moving forward brings more clarity, which makes it simpler to maintain your focus and resolve until you have attained your final goal.

2.

ACCEPT CHANGE

Nothing strikes me as more profound than the idea that a man can change his life by altering his thinking.

Your thoughts are like seeds that you plant in the garden of your mind, and whatever you plant there will undoubtedly grow and bear fruit. I advise you to sow the seeds of faith, prosperity, hope, and success. Only when you are thinking correctly can your actions be correctly thought out.

Rarely does someone excel at something they are not passionate about. It is feasible, but it wouldn't be very enjoyable.

Find your superpower-the thing you excel at both personally and professionally and that comes naturally—and make the decision to develop it.

Find YOUR thing and decide to become excellent at it—we don't have to be the best at everything!

Knowing WHY you pursue your passion, what you enjoy about it, and what benefits you derive from it, is always helpful. What does it do to you? What effect do you have on others or can you have?

The path to greatness will occasionally be tough and exhausting, but it will also be enjoyable and always more meaningful when your "Why" has an influence on others as well as on yourself. Your "Why" might have an effect on your team members, coworkers, employees, a problem in your community, or a problem that you have previously suffered with and now have the chance to solve.

Accept change and use it as an opportunity to advance.

3.

POSITIVITY

HAVE CONFIDENCE AND SELF-BELIEF

You are correct, regardless of whether you believe you can or cannot.Every action has a thought before it.

When you think positively, you will automatically feel more inspired to take action on your goals, which will help you advance and succeed.

Positive thinking has the potential to change your life. Have faith in your abilities and yourself.

If it's difficult for you to believe in yourself, compile a list of all your strengths.

Gaining self-confidence and learning to believe in yourself is one of the best strategies to achieve success.

Greater self-confidence encourages you and provides you the courage to take action on your goals. When you're feeling down, remember your successes and the time, skills, talents, and strengths you have that will enable you to achieve more.

You have the strength to continue till you reach your objectives when you have confidence in your capacity to do so. Even scientific research demonstrates that being upbeat and actively attempting to decrease negative thoughts can be beneficial to your health. Even among those who have a family history of cardiac issues, positive thinkers are 30% less likely than negative thinkers to experience a heart attack.

Being upbeat reduces stress, guards against discouragement, and improves coping mechanisms for when things get tough.

Consider smiling more frequently, using comedy in your life, engaging in positive self-talk, and making a list of the positive parts of a difficult circumstance as ways to help you maintain your positive outlook. Make an effort to surround oneself at home and at work with positive people, images, music, books, podcasts, and settings.

There are frequently just self-imposed restrictions on what you can accomplish, possess, or be.

True success is so much simpler and more likely to happen once you make the firm, unambiguous decision to alter your life by letting go of all mental constraints and devoting your entire being to the attainment of some lofty objective. Before you can succeed, you must be confident in your abilities.

Success must be something you anticipate like the upcoming week. You won't take the activities that will ensure your success until you are convinced of it. Prior to experiencing, you must first believe.

It would be a tragedy to realize your vision of glory and prosperity only to recall times when you were anxious,

annoyed, disappointed, exhausted, and unpleasant. Consider it, if you experience that while attempting to achieve it.

You can't have it if you can't see it, so have confidence.

Going somewhere you can't see is just as challenging as returning from somewhere you've never been. You need to be very clear about what you want to achieve.

4.

DECIDE AND ESTABLISH SENSIBLE OBJECTIVES.

Destinies are decided by choices. Success starts with a choice; it doesn't start with good fortune or chance; it starts with a choice. Make the choice to succeed, and never back down from it.

Your destiny ultimately depends on the choices you make in this life. Decide to achieve every day because nothing is more important to your success than your everyday decisions.

Set SMART objectives. Remember this saying:
"If you FAIL to PLANNED, You PLAN to FAIL,"

Personal objectives are a necessary component of living a successful life. But frequently, after making some first strides in that direction, our ambitions remain unfulfilled. That can be a result of the way we create objectives.

The greatest and most feasible objectives are SMART objectives. Because they are reasonable, well-considered, and include a timetable, SMART goals are attainable.

Make SMART goals by doing the following:

Create a precise, succinct statement that spells out exactly what you hope to accomplish.

Specify a figure or another way to assess your objective, such as "generate 250 business leads" rather than "get more leads."

Measure the process of your goals,track it down.

Achievable: In order to succeed and maintain your motivation, make sure your goal is difficult but doable.

Relevant: Align your objective with the things that will make you feel successful and content in life.

Time-bound: Establish a deadline for when you will accomplish your goal and establish manageable checkpoints along the route.

You can create a success plan by setting goals that are Specific, Measurable, Attainable, Relevant, and Time-bound.

5.

WILLINGNESS

The ability to be willing is an important aspect of excellence. Being eager and prepared to do something is the state of being willing. It is the readiness to take chances and push oneself to the utmost.

You have a better chance of succeeding at greatness if you are eager to learn, experiment, face challenges, and pursue excellence.

Anyone who wants to succeed must possess the quality of willingness. You need to be prepared to work hard and dedicate yourself to making your vision or dream a reality; simply having one is not enough.

Greatness can never be attained if one is unwilling to put in the effort and take on the challenging jobs. You have the drive and determination to make the extra effort required to achieve your goals when you are willing to take on difficulties and push yourself.

Additionally, being open-minded enables you to concentrate on the good things in life and seek out solutions to any issues that may arise. This may keep you motivated and concentrated as you work to achieve your objectives.

Your willingness is necessary for greatness! To go where others won't, we must be prepared to do and make a sacrifice that others won't. You might give up your social life, spending habits, or even a romance. (due to poor timing).

Never compromise

Some of these things will be easy to give up as you work toward greatness because you firmly believe that you were created to be more, to accomplish more, and to change the world. Other things will be more difficult to ignore...

You will need to maintain your position and explain the value of your journey to a specific person (a friend, lover, or boss) at some point.

We can make compromises, but never to the extent of giving up our dream and our purpose. Regardless of whether you learn to multitask, stay up longer than everyone else, or rise earlier than everyone else.

You must serve your greatness, and the desire to experience the process is the key!

Finally, being eager also enables you to remain receptive to fresh suggestions and opportunities. You could discover that you can use your abilities and skills in ways you never imagined when you take on new challenges.

6.

ACQUIRE KNOWLEDGE

One of the most crucial elements for being great is knowledge. It offers the framework for comprehending and putting the concepts, philosophies, and techniques required for success into practice.

It helps us think critically and come up with original answers to the problems we encounter. It also enables us to see the importance of cooperation and the connectivity of all things.

We can only act decisively and make educated decisions when we are well-informed. It instills in us the courage to take chances and overcome challenges that stand in our way. It gives us the knowledge and tools we need to solve issues and advance.

The key to realizing our potential is knowledge. We can realize our potential for greatness in our careers, interpersonal relationships, and communities by learning the appropriate knowledge. The foundation that enables us to achieve our goals and improve as individuals is knowledge.

Knowledge acquisition and application are ongoing processes that need to be actively pursued.

To learn and advance, we must be ready to take chances, make inquiries, and put in the effort required.

Additionally, we must be receptive to criticism and ready to make changes as we go.

The power of knowledge! It is your responsibility to master YOUR trade completely.

Discover more about the endeavor you wish to pursue, then master it. Whatever your idea of greatness is, become an expert at what you do! Remember... Confidence is born from competence!

Never Stop Learning

In your personal or professional life, try to learn something new every day.

Learning is the foundation of growth, so if you want to achieve, make it a daily priority to learn as much as you can. You will succeed in life if you commit your time to learning new things constantly.

A lifelong learner takes the effort to advance their own development and pursue new knowledge. Your quality of life will increase and you will be exposed to more chances that can provide you contentment and happiness if you are always learning new things.

7.

APPLICATION

Without evidence, potential will eventually mean nothing! You can be the most capable and knowledgeable person on earth.

However, the honor will go to the individual who goes out and proves it at work, home, school, or in their sport!

Only by APPLYING what you have learned and practiced can you become great.

Don't be scared to try, even if you fail; the alternative is to not try at all, or to try but not give your all, which will always result in regret.

8.

START IMMEDIATELY!

There is no better time to begin than now! Many people will postpone starting their path to greatness until they believe the timing is appropriate. Life travels quickly, and you never know what's around the next bend. You can't wait another second to define greatness! Whether you start large or small, in a leap or a tiny step, just get started right away, keep at it, and have fun!

Despite the pursuit of your ideal of greatness, keep in mind that YOU are already exceptional! Enjoy everything unique and wonderful about you because loving yourself will make the journey much more enjoyable.

Put in more effort than anyone else!

It's not necessary to possess exceptional brains or flawless appearance. Because you continue to work after everyone else has gone to bed, you can succeed.

Make it a habit to start with the most challenging, crucial activity. Ask yourself, "What would make the biggest difference in my success overall if I only accomplish one thing today?"

Use the same logic to achieve the objectives you have set for yourself. Which are more crucial for long-term contentment and happiness? Prioritize them first.

Greatness demands a lot of work...Don't give up, therefore. If you continue to work at the plow, your harvest will undoubtedly come if your hand is steady.

"The artist is nothing without the gift, but the gift is nothing without work," stated Emile Zola.

9.

REMAIN CONSISTENT, QUIT TRYING TO FIND SHORTCUTS

How many times have you started something but failed to finish it?

You must develop the ability to maintain consistency and keep turning up for yourself every day, even on difficult days, if you want to be successful.

Outlining your goal for the following day the night before is one of the finest strategies to maintain consistency.

It is much simpler to keep on track when you have a list of tasks that are clearly defined and a schedule for when you will do them throughout the day.

Keep in mind that sometimes being present for oneself requires taking a break. Or perhaps you need to speak with someone. It could also just mean waking up at the same time even though you don't want to leave your cozy bed.

Success depends on being consistent,But no matter how reliable you are, life could have different ideas.

Always consider what might happen if things don't go as planned if you want to succeed in life. What would be your response and what would you do?

This will help you be prepared and in the correct frame of mind when that time finally comes, allowing you to face the issue head-on and succeed.

Those who seek shortcuts aren't interested in the knowledge, insights, and complex understandings that successful people acquire through their pursuit of achievement in life.

It takes time, patience, and persistence to succeed the old-fashioned way, so if you want to succeed, do it that way.

The secret to success in life is being able to bring out the best in ourselves in practically any situation. Your capacity to adjust and transform your life.

10.

CHANGE YOUR
DEFINITION OF SUCCESS

You've done something that you thought would help you succeed, then. Next, what? Feelings of accomplishment, fulfillment, and enjoyment are all variable through time.So, once you achieve success in one area, go for it elsewhere.

You establish a pattern, a template for personal achievement in your subconscious mind by conquering challenges and attaining one outstanding accomplishment in any area.

Your natural inclination and ambition will be to replicate that achievement in subsequent endeavors you undertake.

In other words, success teaches you how to succeed. The more you accomplish, the more you are capable of. Success increases your self-belief, your determination, and your faith in your ability to succeed the next time and ultimately realize personal success.

To attain a goal in your career, at school, or both, try to capitalize on your momentum from a personal success achievement. You'll eventually produce a synergistic effect and discover that success is easier to come by in all areas.

Examine the next area of your life where you'd like to succeed, and then start working toward that objective!

11.

COMMITMENT AND PERSEVERANCE

Don't Give up when things are Difficult

I promise that Dedication is not redundant with Application. There are a lot of "one-hit wonders" around. in the fields of business, sports, music, and life. This is not a slight against them. Being a "one-hit wonder" is preferable to having no hits, because "one-hit wonders" are remembered.

However, many people might become content and complacent after experiencing success and grandeur. It's not just failure that can be terrifying. success has defeated its fair share of individuals, groups, and businesses.

After you have achieved your goal, remain committed to your vision. You shouldn't concentrate on achieving something outstanding... thinking about BEING amazing!

12.

ASSOCIATE WITH OUTSTANDING PEOPLE AND IMPART YOUR KNOWLEDGE TO OTHERS

Find those who inspire and push you. Connect with others who have a great mindset. People you can look up to for Support and not discourage you, Individuals who persevered along the path to success.

Bear in mind the proverb "birds of a feather flock together"

"A good teacher is like a candle - it consumes itself to light the way for others," you should also tell those who are eager to learn.

Build a successful legacy, influence others around you, and the world will be a better place because of your life.

Giving back is a way to express gratitude for what you have by helping others.

BUSINESS IDEAS TO

MAKE MONEY QUICKLY

Sitting down at home doing nothing will not make you great, look for something starting small, you might become the best of it later on.

Here are some business you could get involved in to generate money quickly:

1.Food Truck Business (Meal Prep Service): People can't do without food, although they might not be able to prepare it. Starting a food truck business can be a great way to offer fast food options to customers in busy cities and towns.

This business helps busy people out by preparing meals for them to cook or eat. People pay for the meal plans and ingredients that are sent to their home.

You can save yourself the stress of moving around also by getting a delivery man or using a cab. prepare dishes, send to whoever needs and make your money quickly.

2. Craft Beer Brewery: Craft beer is gaining in popularity and many people are looking for unique craft beer. Starting a craft beer brewery can be a great business opportunity.

3, Event Planning Business: This business involves helping people plan parties, weddings, corporate events, and other special occasions. You can offer a range of services from full-service event planning to day-of planning and coordination if you have a knack for organizing and planning events

4. Home Staging: Home staging is a great way to help people sell their homes faster. It involves creating attractive displays in the home to draw potential buyers.

5. Interior Design: Another way to help people make their homes look great is to offer interior design services.

6. Personal Training: If you're a fitness enthusiast, you can help people reach their health and fitness goals by becoming a personal trainer.

7. Car Detailing and Auto repairs: Car detailing is a great way to help people keep their vehicles looking great. Auto repair is a great business to get into if you have a knack for fixing cars.

8. Pet Sitting: If you're an animal lover, pet sitting can be a great business to get into. People often need someone to take care of their pets while they're away.

9. Handyman Services: Handyman services are always in demand. People often need help with small repairs around the house that they don't have the time or skill to do themselves. You can offer services like plumbing, carpentry, electrical, and landscaping.

You can also keep yourself busy doing this with your laptop and phones and be generating income from the comfort of your home

1. Website and Graphic Design: Graphic design services are in demand for businesses that need logos, advertising materials, and more.

Many businesses need help creating and maintaining their websites. You can offer your services to help them do this.You can also offer additional services such as SEO and content writing.

2. Online Coaching/ Course Creation: Many people are looking for help in various subjects, and offering online tutoring can be a great way to make money.

You can offer your services to help people with specific topics such as fitness, business, or relationships.

If you have knowledge in a certain area, you can create an online course to teach others.

You can offer your services to help people with specific topics such as fitness, business, or relationships.

You can offer one-on-one coaching, group coaching, or online courses.

3. Freelance Writing: You can offer your services as a freelance writer to write articles, blog posts, web content, and more.

4. Copywriting: If you have a knack for writing compelling copy, you can offer your services to businesses to help them craft effective content for their products or services.

5. Social Media Consulting: If you are an expert in social media, you can offer your services to help businesses grow their social media presence.

You can help them create content, manage campaigns, and measure results.

6. Mobile App Development: If you have the skills to develop mobile apps, you can offer your services to build apps for businesses or individual clients.

Creating apps for phones and tablets can be a lucrative business. People need apps for everything from entertainment to business productivity.

7. Social Media Marketing Agency: With businesses increasingly relying on social media for marketing, a social media marketing agency can be a great business opportunity. It can help businesses reach a larger audience and increase their sales.

Businesses need help managing their social media accounts. You can offer your services to help them do this

8. Virtual Assistant: You can offer your services as a virtual assistant to help business owners with tasks such as scheduling appointments, data entry, researching potential clients, customers, managing emails and more.

Don't spend lavishly, invest now and enjoy later!
You can invest in any of the following to keep your money growing

1. Mutual Funds: A mutual fund is a type of investment vehicle that pools together money from multiple investors and invests in a variety of assets, such as stocks, bonds and money market instruments. The fund is managed by a professional fund manager who makes decisions about what assets to buy and sell.

2. Real Estate Investment Trusts (REITs): A real estate investment trust (REIT) is a type of investment vehicle that invests in income-producing real estate.

REITs typically invest in a variety of property types, such as office buildings, shopping centers, apartments, and warehouses.

You can purchase properties for rental income or flipping. You can also partner with other investors to increase your capital and diversify your investments.

3. Exchange Traded Funds (ETFs): An exchange-traded fund (ETF) is an investment fund traded on stock exchanges, much like stocks.

An ETF holds assets such as stocks, commodities, or bonds, and trades close to its net asset value over the course of the trading day.

4. Stocks: Stocks are a type of investment that involves the buying and selling of shares of a particular company. When you buy a stock, you become a part-owner of the company and are entitled to a portion of the company's profits

5. Cryptocurrency: Cryptocurrency is a digital asset or virtual currency that is secured by cryptography, which makes it nearly impossible to counterfeit or double-spend.

Cryptocurrency is decentralized, meaning it is not issued or regulated by any government or central bank.
It operates on a distributed public ledger called a blockchain, which records and verifies all transactions.its one of the best you can invest your money in.

6. Commodities: These are physical goods such as gold, silver, oil, and wheat. They are traded on commodity exchanges, and their prices are determined by the forces of supply and demand.

Investors typically buy and sell commodities in the form of futures contracts, which are agreements to buy or sell a certain amount of a commodity at a specific price and date in the future.

7. Forex trading, also known as foreign exchange trading, is the buying and selling of currencies in the global market continue writing please

Forex trading is conducted over the counter (OTC), meaning that traders buy and sell currencies from one another rather than through an exchange. This allows traders to take advantage of the highly liquid and volatile nature of the forex market, as well as the opportunity to benefit from small price movements.

Forex trading can be extremely profitable, but it requires a great deal of skill and knowledge.

CONCLUSION

The journey to greatness starts with the first step. You now have the 12 steps to success in your hands. It is up to you to apply these steps and create the greatness you desire.

As you make progress, you will find that the journey is rewarding and liberating. You have the power to shape your future and create the life you've always dreamed of.

The 12 steps to greatness are a beacon of hope that will guide you to success. So take your first step, and never look back!

- Get angry with your present situation,
- Be ready to accept a change,
- Believe in yourself, be self-confident.
- Make Decisions and set smart goals.

- Be willing,
- Go on and acquire knowledge,
- make use of the knowledge,
- Start now,
- Stop looking for shortcuts
- Change your definition of success
- Be committed and
- Associate with people with Great mindsets

Make progress each day, and be proud of what you have achieved. You have the power to achieve greatness and make your dreams a reality. Every step you take is one step closer to greatness. All that is left is for you to make it happen.

Continue your journey to greatness and create the life of your dream. you have the power to make your success a reality. Believe in yourself, trust the process, and never give up on your dreams.

It is time for you to make your mark and become the great person you were meant to be. Take the first step, and unlock your true potential!